When I'm At Work

Postman

Written by Sue Barraclough
Photography by Chris Fairclough

FRANKLIN WATTS
LONDON • SYDNEY

This Edition 2010
First published in 2006 by Franklin Watts
338 Euston Road, London NW1 3BH

Franklin Watts Australia
Level 17 /207 Kent Street
Sydney, NSW 2000

© 2006 Franklin Watts

Editor: Adrian Cole
Designer: Jemima Lumley
Art direction: Jonathan Hair
Photography: Chris Fairclough

The publisher wishes to thank Roger, Steve, Nick, Dean and all the staff
at the Royal Mail Tunbridge Wells

A CIP catalogue record for this book is available from the
British Library

Dewey Classification Number: 383'.49

ISBN 978 0 7496 9665 8

Printed in China

Franklin Watts is a division of Hachette Children's Books,
an Hachette UK company.
www.hachette.co.uk

Contents

I am a postman 6

Starting work 8

Sorting the post 10

Loading my van 12

Driving my van 14

From house to house 16

Special deliveries 18

Delivering and collecting 20

Emptying a post box 22

Finishing work 24

Postal equipment 26

Sending letters 28

Glossary and index 30

My name is Roger. I am a postman. I sort all the letters and parcels for my round, then I deliver them in my van. I collect post from post boxes, too.

I spend part of my day at the delivery office. This is a building where all the post for my area is stored and sorted.

Starting work

Post comes in all night from sorting offices. When I arrive at work, all the trolleys have been lined up so the bags of post can be emptied and sorted quickly.

I collect letters from another part of the office. I take them back to my sorting frame and sort them out. Each address has a different section in the frame.

Sorting the post

When I have finished sorting, I put all the letters into bundles.

Then I go to a different part of the delivery office and collect the parcels.

I put the bundles into boxes. Then I load the boxes and parcels into a trolley and push it outside to my van.

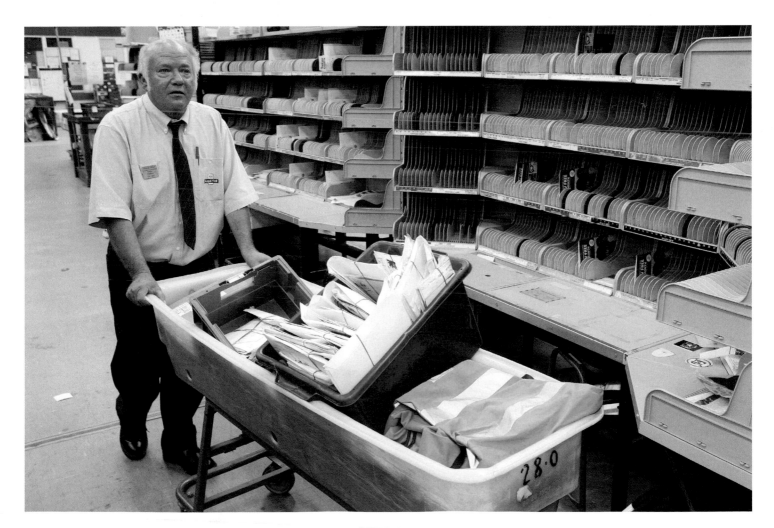

I load all the post into the back of my van. I organise it carefully so I can find it easily on my round.

Then I am ready to go. Other postal workers set off on foot, on bicycles and mopeds, as well as in vans.

Driving my van

I need a van because my round is in the country. I have to drive a long way each day.

At each stop, I find the right bundle in the back of the van. Then I take the post to the house.

I climb back into my van and drive to the next house. There is still a lot more post to deliver.

From house to house

I walk up to each house. Most of the time I post letters through the letterboxes in each door.

But sometimes people wait for their post, especially if it is their birthday! People also wait for other important post

Special deliveries

Some letters and parcels are urgent
or precious. Someone at the address has
to sign to show they have received them.

If no-one is in to sign for the special delivery, I leave a card to let them know I tried to deliver it. Then I take the letter or parcel back to the delivery office.

Delivering and collecting

I deliver post to some offices on my round. Each office usually has a special bag for their post. They get a lot of letters and parcels every day.

When I deliver post to an office, I also collect the letters that they want to send. Then I drive to the next stop on my round.

Emptying a post box

I empty post boxes, too. I unlock the post box and put all the letters into a grey post bag. I load the bag into my van.

When I have finished my round, I drive back
to the delivery office. At the delivery office, I
drop off any post bags I have collected.

Finishing work

Postal workers are finishing their rounds. I put special deliveries that I couldn't deliver in the office. They are stored there until they are collected.

My round is finished. All the vans are parked in the yard, ready for work tomorrow. I sign out and it is time to go home.

Postal equipment

A **sorting frame** is used by postal workers to sort the post for each round. The shelves have different sections labelled with people's addresses.

Post bags are made of strong, waterproof material.

All postal workers wear **high visibility gear** in the delivery office yard and out on their rounds, so people can see them clearly.

Elastic bands hold letters in bundles. Red ones are now mainly used, instead of brown ones. Birds tried to eat any brown ones that were dropped because they thought they were worms.

The **post van** has plenty of room in the back to carry all the post.

Sending letters

Roger works for a company called Royal Mail. Royal Mail sort and deliver millions of letters, parcels and packages every day. Post is delivered on foot and in lorries, vans, mopeds and on bikes.

This post bus is used to deliver and collect letters, and to pick up and drop off passengers too.

Help your postman or postwoman by:

• Writing the address clearly.

• Always using the postcode.

• Wrapping parcels carefully.

postcode

Glossary and index

Delivery office - a large building where post arrives to be stored and sorted. Post vans, bicycles and mopeds are also kept there. **Pages 7, 19, 23, 24.**

Equipment - things you need to do a task. **Pages 26-27.**

Letters - envelopes containing paper or card. **Pages 6, 8, 10, 16, 17, 19, 22.**

Parcels - big packages containing things too large to fit into an envelope. **Pages 10, 11, 19.**

Post box - a special container for post. Post boxes are usually coloured red so that they are easy to see. They are emptied several times each day by postal workers. **Pages 6, 22.**

Round - the route followed by postal workers to deliver and collect post. **Pages 9, 26**

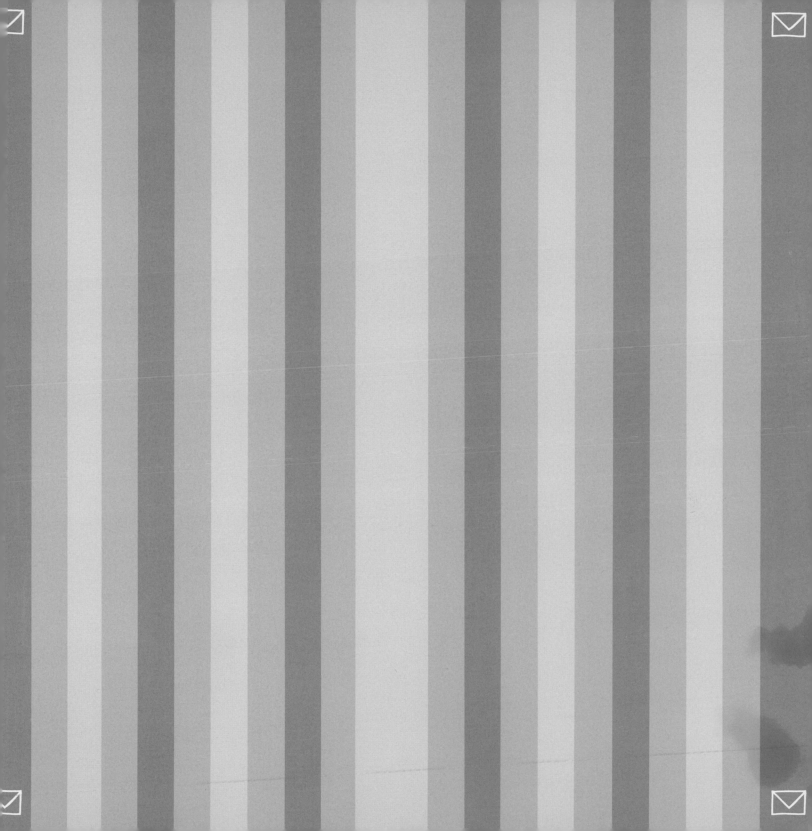